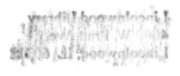

Cultural Traditions in

the

United States

Molly
Aloian

Crabtree Publishing Company

www.crabtreebooks.com

Crabtree Publishing Company

www.crabtreebooks.com

Author: Molly Aloian
Publishing plan research and development:
   Reagan Miller
Editor: Kelly Spence
Proofreader: Marcia Abramson, Wendy Scavuzzo
Indexer: Wendy Scavuzzo
Design: Tibor Choleva
Photo research: Melissa McClellan
Production coordinator and prepress technician:
   Tammy McGarr
Print coordinator: Margaret Amy Salter

Produced and Designed by BlueAppleWorks Inc.

Cover: Rock guitar (left center); Zoloio Almonte bats during an
Eastern League baseball game (center); Manhattan Skyline and
The Statue of Liberty at Night, New York City (background);
eagle (top left); Chevrolet Corvette Roadster (bottom right);
The Statue of Liberty, New York City (right center);
Hot Dog (bottom left)

Title page: Boy standing in front of American Flag

Photographs:
Dreamstime: © Sergeyussr: page 1 (background); © Sonya Etchison:
   page 1; © Orhan Çam: page 4 (top); © Dcarto: page 4 (bottom);
Keystone Press: ©ZUMAPRESS.com: page 20
Library of Congress: page 21
Shutterstock: © Elnur cover (left center); © Aspen Photo cover
   (center); © Joshua Haviv cover (background); © DM7 cover (top
   left); © Digital Media Pro cover (bottom right); © dibrova cover
   (right center); © Oliver Hoffmann cover (bottom left); © Junial
   Enterprises: page 5 (top); © Blend Images: page 5 (bottom);
   © a katz: pages 6, 22; © ZEF: page 7 (top); © ChameleonsEye: page 7
   (bottom); © Rena Schild: page 9; © EPG_EuroPhotoGraphics: page 9
   (insert); © Gema Duran: page 10 (left); © gary yim: page 10 (right);
   © Mike Flippo: page 11 (right); © Natalia Bratslavsky: page 11 (left);
   © littleny: page 12; © Victorian Traditions: page 13; © thatsmymop:
   page 13 (inset); © jorisvo: page 14; © oliveromg: page 15 (top);
   © Hang Dinh: page 16; © Orhan Cam: page 17; © Frontpage: page
   18; © Pete Pahham: page 18 (inset); © Frances L Fruit: page 19;
   © wavebreakmedia: page 20 (inset); © Holger Wulschlaeger: page
   22 (inset); © Digital Media Pro: page 23; © Monkey Business
   Images: page 24 (bottom), 28; © picturepartners: page 24 (top);
   © Rockvilepikephotographs: page 25 (top); © Joakim Lloyd Raboff:
   page 25 (bottom); © lev radin: pages 26, 27 (top); © Anthony
   Correia: page 27 (bottom); © Tatiana Volgutova: pages 28–29
   (background); © lev radin: page 29; © Andrew F. Kazmierski: page
   30 (bottom); © Adam Harner: page 30 (inset); © oliveromg: page 31
   (top); © pilipphoto: page 31 (bottom)
Wikimedia Commons: The New York Times: page 27

Library and Archives Canada Cataloguing in Publication

Aloian, Molly, author
     Cultural traditions in the United States / Molly Aloian.

(Cultural traditions in my world)
Includes index.
Issued in print and electronic formats.
ISBN 978-0-7787-0305-1 (bound).--ISBN 978-0-7787-0317-4 (pbk.).--
ISBN 978-1-4271-7489-5 (html).--ISBN 978-1-4271-7495-6 (pdf)

     1. Holidays--United States--Juvenile literature. 2. United States--
Social life and customs--Juvenile literature. I. Title. II. Series: Cultural
traditions in my world

GT4803.A56 2014   j394.26973   C2014-900915-1
                                             C2014-900916-X

Library of Congress Cataloging-in-Publication Data

Aloian, Molly.
  Cultural traditions in the United States / Molly Aloian.
       pages cm. -- (Cultural traditions in my world)
  Includes index.
  ISBN 978-0-7787-0305-1 (reinforced library binding : alk. paper) -- ISBN 978-0-
7787-0317-4 (pbk. : alk. paper) -- ISBN 978-1-4271-7495-6 (electronic pdf : alk.
paper) -- ISBN 978-1-4271-7489-5 (electronic html : alk. paper)
 1. Holidays--United States--Juvenile literature. 2. Festivals--United States--
Juvenile literature. 3. United States--Social life and customs--Juvenile
literature. I. Title.

  GT4803.A636 2014
  394.26973--dc23
                                             2014005120

Crabtree Publishing Company

www.crabtreebooks.com   1-800-387-7650

Printed in the USA/052014/SN20140313

Published in Canada
Crabtree Publishing
616 Welland Ave.
St. Catharines, ON
L2M 5V6

Published in the United States
Crabtree Publishing
PMB 59051
350 Fifth Avenue, 59th Floor
New York, New York 10118

Published in the United Kingdom
Crabtree Publishing
Maritime House
Basin Road North, Hove
BN41 1WR

Published in Australia
Crabtree Publishing
3 Charles Street
Coburg North
VIC 3058

Contents

Welcome to the United States

Over 300 million people live in the United States. Many of these people were born in America, but some are **immigrants** from other countries. The different religions, traditions, and **races** of the United States people have helped create a unique American culture.

Did You Know?
Washington, D.C., is the capital city of the United States. There are 50 states that make up the United States, including Alaska and the island of Hawaii.

4

American families and friends gather together to celebrate events such as weddings and birthdays. Often these events include cake and presents.

Cultural traditions are holidays, festivals, special days, and customs that groups of people celebrate. Some are religious and others honor an important day in history. In the United States, some holidays are celebrated across the country. Others are only celebrated by a particular state or group of people. This book looks at many of the celebrations that take place during the year across the United States.

5

Happy New Year!

Each year on December 31, many Americans celebrate New Year's Eve. At midnight, people reflect on the year that has passed and welcome the new year ahead. Family and friends celebrate together with parties, music, dancing, parades, and fireworks. New Year's Day on January 1 is a national holiday. Many people have the day off school and work.

Each year, one million people countdown to midnight in Times Square in New York City. Millions more watch the party on television.

Hoppin' John is a popular Southern dish eaten on New Year's Day. It is usually made with peas, rice, beans, and pork.

In some Southern states, eating black-eyed peas on New Year's Day is a popular tradition. It is believed if a person eats black-eyed peas on this day, they will have good luck and good fortune during the new year.

Did You Know?
Many Chinese Americans celebrate Chinese New Year in January or February. There are parades featuring colorful floats, firecrackers, dancing, and fireworks.

Martin Luther King, Jr. Day

On the third Monday of every January, Americans honor Martin Luther King, Jr. Martin Luther King, Jr. was an important African-American **civil rights** leader. He lived from 1929 to 1968. Schools and businesses are closed so that people can spend the day remembering and celebrating his life and achievements.

Did You Know?
Martin Luther King, Jr. is best known for his famous "I Have A Dream" speech, that he made in 1963 from the steps of the Lincoln Memorial in Washington, D.C.

Many children march in parades on Martin Luther King, Jr. Day. In school, they learn about his fight for equality.

Martin Luther King, Jr. Day is a day to learn about and promote equal rights for all people. His **legacy** continues to inspire many people to spread his message of love, peace, and equality around the world.

Mardi Gras and Shrove Tuesday

In the United States, Mardi Gras falls during February or March. This holiday is also called Shrove Tuesday. Shrove Tuesday is the day before the start of **Lent**, which is a period of **fasting** in the Christian religion. While many people celebrate this day for religious reasons, the fun traditions of Mardi Gras are enjoyed by all Americans.

During Mardi Gras, people wear costumes and colorful beads (above). They also eat sweets such as the King's Cake (left).

In French, Mardi Gras means "Fat Tuesday." On this day, people feast on rich, fatty foods, and wear masks and costumes. There are large Mardi Gras parades, festivals, and celebrations across the United States. The most well-known Mardi Gras parade takes place in New Orleans, Louisiana, where Mardi Gras is a state holiday.

Did You Know?
Purple, green, and gold are the official colors of Mardi Gras. Purple represents justice, green represents faith, and gold represents power.

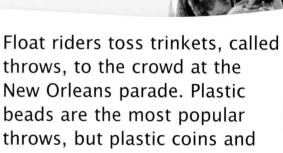

Float riders toss trinkets, called throws, to the crowd at the New Orleans parade. Plastic beads are the most popular throws, but plastic coins and cups are also tossed.

Presidents' Day

On the third Monday of February, many Americans celebrate Presidents' Day, also called Washington's Birthday. This national holiday honors and remembers past presidents of the United States. Two important presidents, George Washington and Abraham Lincoln, are especially honored on this day.

The Federal Hall National Memorial in New York City is a popular spot to visit on Washington's birthday. It was the first home of the U.S. government. George Washington was sworn in as president here.

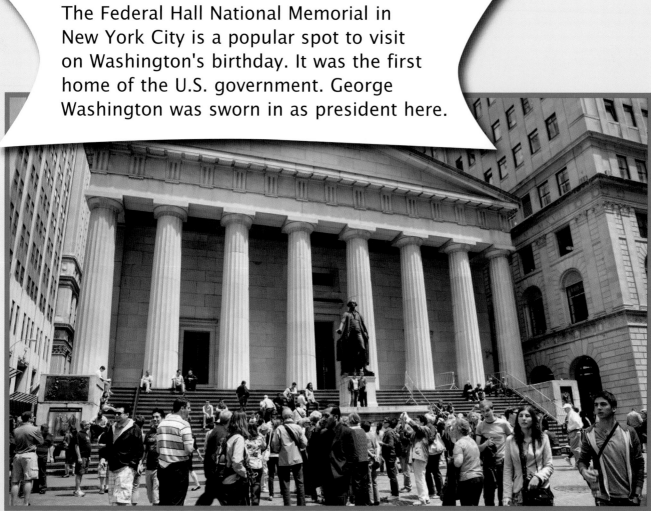

Did You Know?
George Washington's first term as president was from 1789 to 1793. His second term was from 1793 to 1797. He is often called "the Father of Our Country."

President Abraham Lincoln is remembered for his great leadership during the American Civil War.

In the weeks or days leading up to the holiday, teachers often organize events and lessons about the presidents of the United States, especially George Washington. There are also special ceremonies held to honor **veterans**.

Good Friday and Easter

Easter falls in March or April. Many Christians celebrate Good Friday two days before Easter. On Good Friday, people go to special church services to mourn the death of Jesus Christ. On Easter Sunday, services are held celebrating Christ's **resurrection**. People also celebrate Easter with family and friends by sharing a special meal.

This church's stained glass window shows how Jesus Christ died on a cross.

Easter eggs are painted bright colors so they are easy to find on an egg hunt!

Did You Know?
In the Egg Roll, children push a hard-boiled egg across the lawn of the White House with a spoon. Each child receives a wooden egg signed by the President and First Lady as a souvenir.

Easter egg hunts and decorating Easter eggs are other popular Easter activities. The **White House** Easter Egg Roll has been an Easter tradition in the United States since 1878. It is held the Monday after Easter.

Memorial Day

On the last Monday in May, Americans have the day off work and school to commemorate all the people who have died during military service for the United States. Many people visit cemeteries and war memorials on Memorial Day. In national cemeteries, people place American flags on the graves of those who have died. It is also customary to fly the American flag at half-mast, or halfway up the flag pole, from dawn until noon on Memorial Day.

All over the country, people bring flowers and flags to war memorials.

Did You Know?
At three o'clock in the afternoon, Americans observe the National Moment of Silence. During this time, people reflect on the brave heroes who fought and died in military service for their country.

This statue in Washington, D.C., shows soldiers raising the flag at Iwo Jima during World War II. It honors soldiers of the US Marine Corps who died while fighting for their country.

17

Independence Day

On Independence Day, also known as the Fourth of July, Americans celebrate the day the United States officially became its own country. On this day in 1776, the 13 **colonies** signed the Declaration of Independence to declare their official independence from British rule.

People fill the National Mall in Washington, D.C., for one of the largest Independence Day celebrations in the United States.

Scout troops march in Independence Day parades all over the country.

Independence Day celebrations include fireworks, parades, barbecues, carnivals, fairs, picnics, and special political speeches and ceremonies. People decorate with red, white, and blue streamers and balloons, and wear red, white, and blue clothing, which are the colors of the American flag. American flags fly everywhere on Independence Day.

Did You Know?
On June 14, Flag Day is celebrated across the United States. The American flag is nicknamed the "Stars and Stripes." Each star represents one of the 50 states and the 13 stripes represent the colonies that became states when the country's independence was declared from Britain.

Labor Day

Americans celebrate Labor Day on the first Monday of September. It is a celebration of the American workforce and is a day to honor the many important **economic** achievements of workers in the United States.

Workers and their families march for health care changes during a recent Labor Day Parade in Detroit.

Did You Know?
The Labor Day long weekend marks the end of summer for many people. In some states, people enjoy visiting cottages and the beach before the fall begins.

In the 1880s, Labor Day was designated as the day for workers to ask for better working conditions or pay increases. Workers fought for their rights on Labor Day. They fought for eight hours of work, eight hours for recreation, and eight hours for rest. Today, this holiday commemorates the beginning of the eight-hour workday.

Labor Day parades started in New York City and spread across the country. These women in a parade in New York are fighting for trade unions that will help them get higher pay and better working conditions.

Columbus Day and Native American Day

On Columbus Day, which is the second Monday of October, many people commemorate Christopher Columbus' arrival to the Americas on October 12, 1492. People go to special services, parades, and other activities throughout towns and cities and celebrate Columbus' long voyage from Europe across the Atlantic Ocean.

Columbus Day celebrations may include a visit from a replica, or copy, of one of the famous explorer's three ships. This one is the *Santa Maria*. People can tour and even sail on the ship!

A band plays in the Columbus Day Parade in New York City. It is believed to be the world's largest Columbus Day event.

Members of the San Manuel Indian Band celebrate with costumes and dancing at a powwow, a traditional Native American social gathering.

People in some states do not celebrate Columbus Day. Instead, they celebrate Native American Day, or **Indigenous** Peoples' Day. Some cities celebrate with ceremonies featuring music, traditional clothing, dancing, food, and crafts. It is a day to celebrate the heritage of Native cultures for both Native people and non-Native people.

Did You Know?
Some people do not celebrate Columbus Day because the many European **settlers** that came to the Americas nearly wiped out the Native peoples who had been living there for thousands of years.

Happy Halloween!

Americans celebrate Halloween on October 31 each year. The tradition of Halloween was brought to the United States by Scottish and Irish immigrants. Today, kids dress up in costumes and go out trick-or-treating. They knock on the doors of their neighbors and say, "Trick-or-treat!" and then receive candy or other treats.

Kids collect some Halloween treats. Chocolate candy is the most popular!

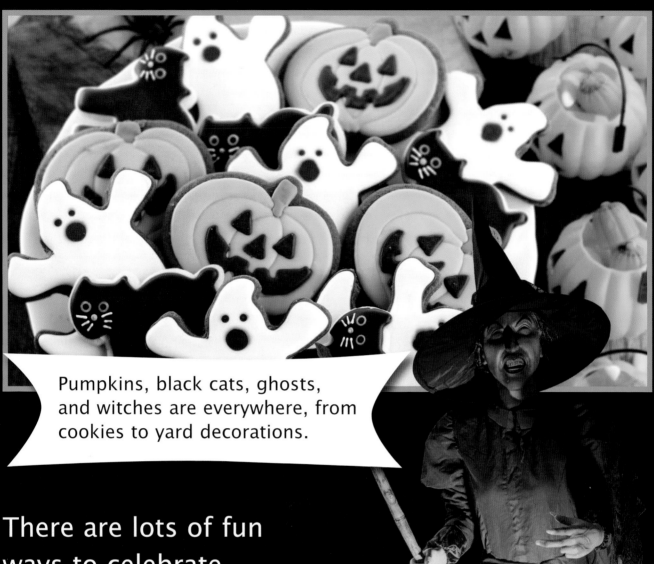

Pumpkins, black cats, ghosts, and witches are everywhere, from cookies to yard decorations.

There are lots of fun ways to celebrate Halloween. In the United States, people go to costume parties, visit haunted houses or pumpkin patches, or go to the theater to watch scary Halloween movies.

Did You Know?
According to ancient **Celtic** beliefs, Halloween is the only night of the year when spirits of the dead can cross over into the world of the living.

Veterans Day

Veterans Day is an important day in the United States. On November 11 each year, people remember and honor the men and women who have served the United States in the military. Americans are thankful to those who have served their country because their bravery and courage helps to protect the freedom and safety of the United States. They gave their lives so other Americans could live in peace.

Current members of the military as well as veterans march in parades all over the United States.

Some Veterans Day events include placing floral wreaths (above). Others are parades that salute veterans (below).

Did You Know?
November 11 is the anniversary of the signing of the **armistice** that ended World War I. People attend parades and church services. There is usually a period of silence lasting two minutes at 11 a.m.

Thanksgiving

On the fourth Thursday of November, Americans celebrate Thanksgiving and the harvest of fall foods. They often spend the long weekend visiting family or friends and eating a traditional Thanksgiving meal of turkey, stuffing, squash, potatoes, and pumpkin pie. Many people go on hikes or nature walks. Others watch football on television. There are also parades and other celebrations that mark the beginning of the Christmas shopping season.

Before eating Thanksgiving dinner, many people give thanks for all their blessings.

The Macy's Thanksgiving Day Parade in New York City is one of the nation's oldest. Philadelphia and Detroit also have had parades for many years.

Did You Know?
Native people held ceremonies and festivals to celebrate the fall harvest long before European explorers and settlers arrived in present-day United States. They celebrated and gave thanks for all the gifts from the land.

Christmas

Many Americans celebrate Christmas on December 25 each year. They celebrate the birth of Jesus Christ. During the Christmas season, people decorate their homes with twinkly lights and hang colorful ornaments on Christmas trees. On Christmas Eve, many people go to church for special Christmas services.

Did You Know?
In the state of Hawaii, Santa Claus, or *Kanakaloka*, brings presents in a canoe instead of a sleigh. People wish their friends and family happy holidays in Hawaiian by saying "Mele Kalikimaka!"

Most U.S. cities and towns are decorated for the holiday season with twinkling lights and giant Christmas trees.

Christmas dinner brings the family together. Parents are off work and kids get a week or more of vacation from school!

Family members exchange gifts and visit with friends and relatives on Christmas Eve or Christmas Day. Many people also enjoy a special festive meal including roast turkey or ham, potatoes, vegetables, cranberry sauce, and gravy. Christmas desserts include cookies decorated with icing, candy canes, pies, tarts, and gingerbread.

Glossary

armistice A pause or stop in fighting brought about by agreement between the two sides

Celtic Relating to a group of people called the Celts who lived in ancient Britain and parts of Europe

civil rights The personal rights of a United States citizen as written in the 13th and 14th amendments to the United States Constitution

colonies Areas of land ruled by another country

economic Relating to the system of producing, buying, and selling goods and services

fasting Going without food

immigrants People who come from one country to live in another country

indigenous Living in a certain area originally

legacy Something a person is remembered for

Lent A period of fasting and regret for one's sins during the 40 weekdays from Ash Wednesday to Easter

races a group of people of common ancestry

resurrection brought back to life after death

settlers People who make their homes in a new region

veterans Former members of the armed forces

White House The home and office of the U.S. president and his wife, the First Lady

Index